RESTLESS
LEAD

BECAUSE YOU WERE MADE FOR MORE

JENNIE ALLEN

W PUBLISHING GROUP

AN IMPRINT OF THOMAS NELSON

Published in Nashville, Tennessee, by W Publishing, an imprint of Thomas Nelson.

Author image © Jessica Taylor. Used with permission.

Typesetting: Crosslin Creative

Thomas Nelson, Inc., titles may be purchased in bulk for educational, business, fund-raising, or sales promotional use. For information, please e-mail SpecialMarkets@ThomasNelson.com.

Unless otherwise noted, Scripture quotations are taken from HOLY BIBLE: NEW INTERNATIONAL VERSION®. © 1973, 1978, 1984, 2011 by Biblica, Inc.™ Used by permission. All rights reserved. Scripture verses marked ESV are taken from THE ENGLISH STANDARD VERSION. © 2001 by Crossway Bibles, a division of Good News Publishers.

ISBN 978-0-8499-2283-1

Printed in the United States of America

16 17 RRD 6 5 4 3

CONTENTS

INTRODUCTION

LEADERS,

I am excited to partner with you in your efforts to pour into the lives of women! I pray that these few short pages will help to equip and prepare you to lead this study. Many of you may have led plenty of groups in the past, or perhaps this is the first you've led. Whichever the case, this is a spiritual calling and you are entering spiritual places with these women—and spiritual callings and places need spiritual power.

My husband, Zac, always says, "Changed lives, change lives." If you are not first aware of your own need for life change, the women around you won't see their need. If you allow God into the inner struggles of your heart, the women following you will be much more likely to let him into theirs. These women do not need to see bright and shiny, perfectly poised people; they need to see people who are a mess and daily dependent on God for their hope and strength.

So, what are we going to do together here?

Every single one of us is designed to fit into a unique space with unique offerings. God's will for each one of us will look different. There is a framework within the commandments of Scripture, and within it we are free to create lives reflecting God and his passions here.

First, we are going to chase down and tackle some of what is holding us back from obedience. Then, in part two, we are going to try to get our heads around God and what he is doing on this earth. Then we will consider exactly what pieces of life God has given you to participate in his story. In part three, we will explore what it looks like to live out our purposes. Throughout, we will look at these heart issues in the life of Joseph, a man who dreamed God's dreams and lived his part in God's story. Joseph's life, told of throughout Genesis 37 to 50, is the story of a life that at times must have felt wasted, and yet God was working in every moment that felt mundane and unfair and dark.

In the end, this is a book about God. It's about the moment at the end of our lives when we will see him. It's about facing the God of the universe and celebrating with him about the life and resources he gave us while we were here.

And because we all want that moment to go well, this is a book about discovering ourselves and getting over ourselves all at the same time. It's about being brave enough to imagine a better world and how we may be used to make it that way. It's about changing the world and changing diapers. About fears and suffering and joy and gifts. About all that is within our control and how nothing is in our control. It's about vision and obedience.

This is a book about spending our lives completely on the glory of God.

We want to know: "What does God want me to do while I am here?" The answer seems hidden and complicated, yet we must go after it. We must not get to heaven and realize we have lived for all the wrong things.

We must not waste our lives. Let's go.

WHAT'S IN THE BOX

Each *Restless* kit includes:

STUDY. A copy of the study guide (each member of your group will need her own study guide). Additional study guides can be purchased separately (ISBN: 978-0-8499-2236-7).

SEE. A DVD with eight sessions

ASK. A set of conversation cards

LEAD. A copy of the leader's guide

If you have a large group of women and need to break down into smaller groups during your study times, you may want to purchase additional kits so each group can have access to a leader's guide and a set of Ask conversation cards.

We will discuss how to use each element of this kit on pages 12–16.

THE VISION

1. That God and eternity would get bigger and more real in your lives, and that as they do get bigger, you would feel compelled to live for eternity and Jesus Christ more than this short life. More than anything, I want you to fix your eyes on Jesus and fall more deeply in love with him.

2. That you would feel released and convicted to dream with the many unique threads that God has placed in your lives, and that you would each see how valuable and important your part in building the kingdom of God is.

3. That you would speak life and peace and freedom into each other. That you would encourage each other in your uniqueness rather than judge or condemn the different paths God may have each of us running.

In sum, here it is . . . this is my dream: That we would all fix our eyes on Jesus, throw off the small junk that holds us back, and run our marked races, cheering each other on.

Therefore, since we are surrounded by such a great cloud of witnesses, let us throw off everything that hinders and the sin that so easily entangles. And let us run with perseverance the race marked out for us, fixing our eyes on Jesus, the pioneer and perfecter of faith. For the joy set before him he endured the cross, scorning its shame, and sat down at the right hand of the throne of God. Consider him who endured such opposition from sinners, so that you will not grow weary and lose heart.

HEBREWS 12:1–3

The rest of this leader's guide is aimed at equipping you to point the women of your group to God in ways that will change their lives.

PREPARING YOURSELF TO LEAD A GROUP

1. PRAY: Pray like the world is ending, pray like this is the last chance for people to know him, pray like your lives and futures depend on it, pray like the future of souls in heaven is at stake . . . pray like you need God.

Pray for your women:

:: That God would show them why they are restless, and what their hearts truly long for.

:: That they would feel safe to open up and process.

:: That they would want more of God and that God would meet them.

:: That the conversation would be focused on God.

:: That we would be humble displays of God's grace to these women.

:: That God would come and fall on your time together.

:: That many would come to a saving faith as they see God for who he is.

2. **LEAN ON GOD.** Allow the Holy Spirit to lead every moment together. We have provided you with tools that we will discuss in the next section; however, they are only tools to use as the Spirit leads you and your time together. God will have unique agendas for each of your groups as you depend on him. Lean into your own weakness and into his strength and direction.

When Jesus left his disciples to go back to his Father in heaven, he essentially said, "Don't go anywhere until you have the helper I will send you" (see Acts 1:4–5). That helper was the Holy Spirit. We need to obey that same command. We shouldn't begin until we are doing so with the power of the Holy Spirit within us. He is real and available and waiting to flood our lives and the lives of those around us as we serve and speak. But we have to wait for him to speak, ask him if we should speak and what we should speak, and ask him what to do in different situations. God wants us to need him and to depend on his Spirit. If this is not how you live on a daily basis, begin today.

3. **BE TRANSPARENT.** If you choose not to be vulnerable, no one else will be. If you desire women to feel safe with you and your group, be vulnerable. This is not an optional assignment. This is your calling as you lead these women.

4. LISTEN BUT ALSO LEAD. Listen as women share struggles. Some women are taking a tremendous risk in being vulnerable with you. Protect them by not interrupting but by empathizing instead. Do not feel the need to speak after each person shares. After most women have shared their answers to a question, turn it back to the scripture from the study guide and help them process the truth and hope in their struggles. Avoid lecturing, but do bring the women back to truth.

5. MODEL TRUST. Show your group how you are applying these difficult lessons. Ask God to convict you and lead out with how you are processing change in your own life.

THE STUDY: SESSION TOOLS AND FORMAT

This study is uniquely designed to work in any venue or location. I envision women leading this in their homes, on campuses, even in their workplaces. Church buildings are the traditional format for group Bible studies and *Restless* will be effective within the church walls, but the bigger dream is that women would find this study useful in reaching their friends, neighbors, and coworkers.

Whether you find yourself with 150 women in a church auditorium or with a few neighbors in your living room, this study is designed for small groups of women to process truth within their souls.

Because of the depth of the questions and topics, it is essential your group be small enough to share. A maximum of eight women in each group is ideal, but fewer is preferable. If you are in a larger group, divide into smaller groups with volunteer facilitators. With the help of the leader's guide and the Ask conversation cards, those smaller groups should still prove successful with a little support.

SESSION TOOLS AND HOW TO USE THEM

STUDY. In the first meeting, distribute your groups' study guides (or if women are purchasing on their own, remind them to bring their study guides to the first meeting). The lessons in the study guide (except for the Getting Started lesson) are meant to be completed during the week before coming to the group meeting. Each week begins with a short intro before moving into the portion marked "Study." The Study portion is followed by four application projects, then closing thoughts from me. The Study portion and projects can be completed in one sitting or broken up into smaller parts throughout the week, depending on each individual woman's needs.

These lessons may feel different from studies you have done in the past. They are very interactive. The goal of the curriculum is to lead women to dig deeply into Scripture and uncover how it applies to their lives, to deeply engage the mind and the heart. Projects, stories, and Bible study all play a role. The projects in the study guide will provide several options for applying Scripture. You and your group members may be drawing or journaling or engaging in some other activity in these projects. At the group meeting, discuss your experience in working through the lesson.

SEE. These short, engaging videos are meant to set the tone for your time together, to draw women deeper into Scripture, and to set the stage for transparent sharing. Hopefully, each person has already deeply studied the scriptures for themselves before coming to the group, and the video will provide enough to jump-start a powerful time of reflection and processing how to apply all they have learned in personal study that week.

ASK. These cards provide a unique way of starting deep, honest conversations about what you're chasing after. Each week's cards are labeled with the appropriate lesson title. These should be pulled out after the DVD or teaching time.

1. Lay out the cards for the week, with the questions facing up.

2. Allow each woman to grab her favorite one.

3. Every week, go over the Ground Rules found in the front of the Ask deck of cards.

4. Begin by laying out the Scripture card for that week. Refer back to it as needed for help processing as you share.

5. Take turns having each woman ask the question on her card. Allow time for anyone who wants to share or respond to the question.

6. You may only get through a few of the questions. That is fine.

The goals of the questions are to allow women to reflect on what they have studied and heard and have a chance to share their own hearts. Again, do not be afraid to lead the discussion back to God if it feels like things are getting off topic, but first allow everyone to concisely and clearly communicate their hearts. Several of the cards each week have Scripture on them to help you do that. Pull one of those if you feel the group needs to hear what God says about the issues.

LEAD. This guide serves as a tool to prepare you in leading this study and to encourage you along the way. Refer back to it each week to be aware of the goals for each lesson. The leader's guide will help you effectively point your women to the overarching theme of each lesson and point them to the themes of the study.

SESSION FORMAT

This eight-week study is designed to go deep very quickly. Since women are busy and have full lives, the beauty of this study is it can be led in a living room over a one-hour lunch, or in a church Bible study spread out over two and a half hours. If you have the flexibility, extend the time of sharing in small groups. A frequent complaint is, "We wish we had more time to share." When the group is given deep questions and space to reflect and respond, you'll be surprised how beautiful and plentiful the conversations will be.

These tools are meant to have some flexibility. Here are some suggestions for how to structure your meeting to get the most out of your time together. However, you will be the best judge of what works for your group and the time you have together. Based on your group's needs, choose any combination of going through the questions mixed with reflections from group members' personal study.

HOMEWORK DISCUSSION [20–35 MINUTES]:

After welcoming everyone and opening in prayer, you may choose to begin by having the women discuss their personal reflections as they have worked through the study guide and Scripture that week. If you have more than eight members, break into small groups for this discussion time before reconvening for the video/teaching time.

VIDEO AND/OR TEACHING [VIDEO: 20 MINUTES]:

Watch the DVD to provide a foundation for that week's lesson and to help transition to transparent sharing using the Ask conversation cards. Each video is approximately twenty minutes long. If you are supplying teaching in addition to the videos, we recommend you begin with your teaching and then play the video.

NOTE TO CHURCH GROUPS: Due to the nature of this study, we strongly suggest that each group have no more than eight to twelve women and that you have a kit for each group.

ASK CONVERSATION CARDS [30–75 MINUTES]:

Especially if there are more than eight group members, divide into smaller groups and have women go through the Ask conversation cards. This will be a time of deep sharing and discussion that is important to understanding how to apply all that has been learned that week. If your small group needs an extra deck of Ask cards, they are available for purchase at www.thomasnelson.com.

LEADING YOUR GROUP: TIPS AND THINGS TO WATCH OUT FOR

GUIDING CONVERSATION

You may come across some challenges when leading a group conversation. Normally these challenges fall into two categories. In both situations people will need encouragement and grace from you as a leader. As with everything in this study, seek the Holy Spirit's guidance as you interact with your group members.

1. DOMINATING THE CONVERSATION: If one woman seems to be dominating the conversation or going into detail that makes the rest of the group uncomfortable, gently interrupt her if necessary and thank her for sharing. Avoid embarrassing her in front of the group. Ask if there is anyone else who would like to share in response to the original question asked (not to necessarily respond to the woman who was just speaking). If the problem persists, talk with the woman outside of the group time. Affirm her for her vulnerability and willingness to share and be prepared to refer her for more help if the need arises.

2. NOT SHARING AS MUCH AS THE OTHERS:

If you notice there is a woman who seems to not be as talkative as the others in the group, you may try gently asking for her input directly at some point in the conversation. Some women are naturally shyer than others; don't try to force them into an extroverted role, but do let them know their input is valuable to the group. Remind them of the goals of the study and how being vulnerable with one another is one of the ways God shapes us spiritually. If a woman is just not interested in being in the study and is holding the rest of the group back, meet with her outside the group setting to discuss her further involvement.

Keep in mind that no two women are alike, but keep the best interests of the group in mind as you lead. Encourage group members to follow the Ground Rules for Group Discussion Time (listed below and also found on pages 5–6 in the study guide.) Review these items together as often as needed in order to keep the conversation on track:

:: **BE CONCISE.** Share your answers to the questions while protecting others' time for sharing. Be thoughtful. Don't be afraid to share with the group, but try not to dominate the conversation.

:: **KEEP GROUP MEMBERS' STORIES CONFIDENTIAL.** Many things your group members share are things they are choosing to share with you, not with your husband or other friends. Protect each other by not allowing anything shared in the group to leave the group.

:: **RELY ON SCRIPTURE FOR TRUTH.** We are prone to use conventional, worldly wisdom as truth. While there is value in that, this is not the place. If you feel led to respond, please only respond with God's truth and Word, not "advice."

:: **NO COUNSELING.** Protect the group by not directing all attention on solving one person's problem. This is the place for confessing and discovery and applying truth together as a group. As a group leader, you will be able to direct a woman to more help outside the group time if she needs it.

WHEN TO REFER

Some of the women in your care may be suffering beyond the point you feel able to help. This study may bring the pain of circumstances or behaviors to the surface. To leave women in this state would be more damaging than helpful. Don't try to take on problems you do not feel equipped to handle. If you sense that a woman may need more help, follow up and refer her to someone.

:: Check with your church or pastor for names of trusted Christian counselors. Some major indicators of this need would be: depression, anxiety, thoughts of suicide, abuse, or a broken marriage. These are the obvious ones, but honestly, some women who are stuck in hurt from their past, minor depression, or fear could also benefit from counseling. I believe counseling is beneficial for many. So keep a stash of names for anyone you may feel needs to process further with a professional.

:: Look for the nearest Celebrate Recovery group and offer to attend the first meeting with her (www.celebraterecovery.com).

:: Suggest further resources and help to make a plan for their future growth and well-being.

:: Communicate with the leadership at your church about how to proceed with care.

:: Do not abandon these hurting women in a vulnerable place. This may be the first time they have opened up about painful hurts or patterns. Own their care and see it through. If they have landed in your group, God has assigned them to you for this season, until they are trusted to the care of someone else. Even then, continue to check in on them.

TYPES OF LEARNERS

Hopefully, you will be blessed to be leading this study with a group diverse in age, experience, and style. While the benefits of coming together as a diverse group to discuss God outweigh the challenges by a mile, there are often distinctions in learning styles. Just be aware and consider some of the differences in two types of learning styles that may be represented. (These are obviously generalizations, and each woman as an individual will express her own unique communication style, but in general these are common characteristics.)

EXPERIENTIAL LEARNERS

These are women who are more transparent, don't like anything cheesy, want to go deep quickly, and are passionate. Make a safe environment for them by being transparent yourself and engaging their hearts. These women may not care as much about head knowledge and may care more deeply how knowledge about God applies to their lives. They want to avoid being put in a box. Keep the focus on applying truth to their lives and they will stay engaged.

PRAGMATIC LEARNERS

These women are more accustomed to a traditional, inductive, or precept approach to Bible study. They have a high value for truth and authority but may not place as high a value on the emotional aspects of confessing sin and being vulnerable. To them it may feel unnecessary or dramatic. Keep the focus on the truth of Scripture. These women keep truth in the forefront of their lives and play a valuable role in discipleship.

∗ ∗ ∗

Because this study is different from traditional studies, some women may need more time to get used to the approach. The goal is still to make God big in our lives, to know and love him more, and to deal with sin by instructing with Scripture. These are the goals for all believers; we all just approach them in unique ways to reach unique types of people. I actually wrote this study praying it could reach both types of learners. I am one who lives with a foot in both worlds, trying to apply the deep truths I gained in seminary in an experiential way. I pray that this study would deeply engage the heart and the mind, and that we would be people who worship God in spirit and in truth, not just learning about sin but going to war with it together.

Common struggles like fear, stress, anger, shame, and insecurity are not respecters of age, religion, or income level. These struggles are human. But I have seen that as women are honest about them, we transcend the typical boundaries of Christian and seeker, young and old, single and married, needy and comfortable, coming together and to God in a unique and powerful way.

In the following pages and notes for each *Restless* lesson, I hope I have given you enough guidance that you do not feel lost, but enough freedom to depend on the Holy Spirit. These are only suggestions, but hopefully these notes will help surface themes and goals to guide you through your discussion of group members' homework and through the discussion of the Ask conversation cards. The video, homework, and cards should provide more than enough material for great discussions, but stay on track and be sure people are walking away with hope and truth.

Because you were made for more.

During this first meeting you will be getting to know each other, handing out the study guides, walking through the Instructions and Expectations (found on pages 4–10 of the study guide), walking through the Getting Started lesson (found on pages 11–30 of the study guide), and watching the first video.

Here are some general goals and thoughts for your time together this week:

:: Make the women feel safe.

:: Get to know each other and the things that are making you restless.

:: Set expectations for the study.

:: Have the people in your group go through the Respond section of the introductory lesson and discuss your responses.

:: Instruct group members on how to use the study guide and Ask conversation cards.

:: Reinforce that all of us are restless for something and that God wants us to live our everyday lives in light of eternity. But this is sometimes difficult to do.

:: Introduce Joseph.

LEADER: This first session's suggested format is different from the others since it is your first meeting and there is no homework to review.

VIDEO AND/OR TEACHING

For this first meeting, it is best to begin by watching the video session *Restless*.

DISCUSSION TIME

1. Together take some time to read Instructions and Expectations and the Getting Started lesson in the study guide either aloud or to yourselves and discuss.

2. When you reach page 29 in the Getting Started lesson of the study guide, have participants choose the three things holding you back from dreaming. Give everyone time to think about this and write down in their guide their three things.

3. If you are in a large group, break into small groups and give each person the chance to open up about the three things keeping her from dreaming right now. Leaders, share first and be transparent.

4. After all the women have shared, you may transition to the Ask conversation cards to continue your discussion. The cards for this week are labeled "Restless" on the front. Distribute this week's Ask cards and guide the women to ask and answer the questions on the cards. Review the Ask card instructions together. Remember to begin with the Scripture card and end by stressing the scriptural truth group members can apply to their lives as a result of what they discussed in your group time. Close this discussion in prayer.

Let us throw off everything that hinders and the sin that so easily entangles. And let us run with perseverance the race marked out for us, fixing our eyes on Jesus, the pioneer and perfecter of faith . . . so that you will not grow weary and lose heart.

HEBREWS 12:1–3

GOD'S STORY :: 1

The place where your restless soul meets God is the place where nothing ever feels small again.

MAIN IDEA: We were built to live for this eternal story, even in our everyday mundane lives. Often we forget the weight of the spiritual and miss how God wants us to participate.

This week we will be wrestling with our places in this very big story that God is building. Rather than feeling small in it, help your people to see that this is an honor to be a part of, and it could change the way we view every part of our lives.

Here are some general goals and thoughts for your time together this week:

:: Identify what is difficult to believe about God's story. Encourage open, honest sharing. We all doubt God at times.

:: Dream about how God's story could impact our day-to-day life.

:: Discuss God's love for us in this story. How does that change you?

:: Discuss how this story could and should affect our dreams and hopes for our time here.

MAIN GOAL: That you would be transformed by the story of God and compelled to live for the story of God.

HOMEWORK DISCUSSION

Here are some suggested places to focus as you go over the homework together. Ask the group:

:: Share what you learned as you studied God's work on the earth in Hebrews 10:36–12:3.

:: How did John 17 speak to you based on where you are in your life right now?

:: Discuss your response to Projects 2 and 3.

:: What else did you learn as you studied and interacted with the lesson and Scripture this week?

VIDEO AND/OR TEACHING

Watch video session: *God's Story*

ASK CONVERSATION CARDS

If you are in a large group, break into small groups of five for discussion time using the Ask conversation cards. Distribute this week's Ask cards and guide the women to ask and answer the questions on the cards. Remember to begin with the Scripture card and end by stressing the scriptural truth group members can apply to their lives as a result of what they discussed in your group time. Close this discussion in prayer.

I have brought you glory on earth by finishing the work you gave me to do.

JOHN 17:4

GIFTS :: 2

God has a plan to use your gifts, personality, and work to display himself to your portion of the world.

MAIN IDEA: We each have unique gifts that God wants to reveal and unleash for his glory.

This week we studied the account of Joseph's dreams, and hopefully everyone gained new insight into this familiar story. God equipped Joseph with gifts that were part of his plan, and he has done the same for you.

Here are some general goals and thoughts for your time together this week:

:: Create a restlessness in the women, so that they don't settle for mediocre lives or wasted gifts.

:: Our motive for action must be the glory of God; create a burden in your group members for the glory of God on this earth.

:: What does it look like to live with a single-minded desire to see God and please him?

:: Understand that many of the moments in our lives we have felt most fulfilled likely contain our unique gifts and passions.

:: Identify the things that hold us back from using our gifts.

MAIN GOAL: Identify and name your gifts and dream about how you could use them.

HOMEWORK DISCUSSION

Here are some suggested places to focus as you go over the homework together. Ask the group:

:: Discuss 1 Corinthians 13:1–12. Describe the attributes of love, and how a person's gifts come to life with such love.

:: What are you afraid might happen if you really use your gifts?

:: What was God speaking to you through 1 Corinthians 12?

:: Share your results from Project 4. Have people pair up so that everyone gets to share.

:: What else did you learn as you studied and interacted with the lesson and Scripture this week?

VIDEO AND/OR TEACHING

Watch video session: *Gifts*

ASK CONVERSATION CARDS

If you are in a large group, break into small groups of five for discussion time using the Ask conversation cards. Distribute this week's Ask cards and guide the women to ask and answer the questions on the cards. Remember to begin with the Scripture card and end by stressing the scriptural truth group members can apply to their lives as a result of what they discussed in your group time. Close this discussion in prayer.

Just as a body, though one, has many parts, but all its many parts form one body, so it is with Christ.

1 CORINTHIANS 12:12

SUFFERING :: 3

Out of our pain we could heal our world.

MAIN IDEA: That our sufferings could contain our deepest passions and the things we would most like to see healed around us.

This week we studied a potentially painful subject: suffering. We asked God to heal our hearts and show us the purpose behind our pain.

Here are some general goals and thoughts for your time together this week:

:: To accept, heal, and consider how God may want to move in and through our suffering.

:: To observe how Joseph served through and with his suffering.

:: To consider how our suffering has equipped and matured us.

MAIN GOAL: To uncover and process the moments that we have suffered most and consider how God may want to redeem that for others' healing.

HOMEWORK DISCUSSION

Here are some suggested places to focus as you go over the homework together. Ask the group:

:: As you studied Joseph's suffering this week, what did you learn?

:: What did you uncover as you studied 2 Corinthians 1:3–7 this week?

:: Which project stood out to you most this week?

:: What else did you learn as you studied and interacted with the lesson and Scripture this week?

VIDEO AND/OR TEACHING

Watch video session: *Suffering*

ASK CONVERSATION CARDS

If you are in a large group, break into small groups of five for discussion time using the Ask conversation cards. Distribute this week's Ask cards and guide the women to ask and answer the questions on the cards. Remember to begin with the Scripture card and end by stressing the scriptural truth group members can apply to their lives as a result of what they discussed in your group time. Close this discussion in prayer.

Praise be to the God and Father of our Lord Jesus Christ, the Father of compassion and the God of all comfort, who comforts us in all our troubles, so that we can comfort those in any trouble with the comfort we ourselves receive from God.

2 CORINTHIANS 1:3–4

PLACES :: 4

It's not our places; it's what we do in our places.

MAIN IDEA: Places will never fulfill us, but can serve as the fertile ground for God to make himself known through us.

Here are some general goals and thoughts for your time together this week:

:: Our places are significant because God sets us in them and has work for us to do there.

:: Even so, there is freedom for God to move through us wherever we are.

:: Joseph received his places as God's will and worked hard for God's glory despite severe limitations and suffering.

:: It is not about where we are, but how we execute God's mission for our lives wherever we are.

:: If we would each fulfill God's work for our lives in our spots, the whole earth would be more full of his love and glory.

:: We will never be fully satisfied in any place, except our eternal home with God one day.

MAIN GOAL: Lead people to consider their places and what it would look like to live more intentionally in them.

HOMEWORK DISCUSSION

Here are some suggested places to focus as you go over the homework together. Ask the group:

:: Talk about Joseph's places in Genesis 39 and 40, and discuss his reactions to those places.

:: Look back at Philippians 1:12–26. What did you learn about place?

:: What kind of vision might God have for your places? Discuss Project 1.

:: What else did you learn as you studied and interacted with the lesson and Scripture this week?

VIDEO AND/OR TEACHING

Watch video session: *Places*

ASK CONVERSATION CARDS

If you are in a large group, break into small groups of five for discussion time using the Ask conversation cards. Distribute this week's Ask cards and guide the women to ask and answer the questions on the cards. Remember to begin with the Scripture card and end by stressing the scriptural truth group members can apply to their lives as a result of what they discussed in your group time. Close this discussion in prayer.

For to me, to live is Christ and to die is gain.

PHILIPPIANS 1:21

PEOPLE :: 5

GOD'S STORY

God's economy makes beautiful exchanges: as we give, we grow.

MAIN IDEA: When we run our races, there are people we need and people who need us.

Here are some general goals and thoughts for your time together this week:

:: We need people to encourage us as we run and to remind us of our bigger purposes.

:: We brush shoulders with people who need us, and God wants us to not waste time with them and opportunities to love them well wherever we are.

:: Intentional relationships take time and work and grace. Relationships often break down; it will take a lot of grace to stick with your people.

:: Our greatest purposes are often revealed by those who know us best, and through loving and meeting needs in the people around us.

MAIN GOAL: Identify the need for the right people in your life to help you run your race, and identify the people God has put on your path to love with his love.

HOMEWORK DISCUSSION

Here are some suggested places to focus as you go over the homework together. Ask the group:

:: What did you think of the way Joseph treats people in Genesis 41–45? What stood out about his behavior?

:: What convicted you in Hebrews 10:19–36?

:: Break into pairs and share your charts from Project 1 with each other.

:: What else did you learn as you studied and interacted with the lesson and Scripture this week?

VIDEO AND/OR TEACHING

Watch video session: *People*

ASK CONVERSATION CARDS

If you are in a large group, break into small groups of five for discussion time using the Ask conversation cards. Distribute this week's Ask cards and guide the women to ask and answer the questions on the cards. Remember to begin with the Scripture card and end by stressing the scriptural truth group members can apply to their lives as a result of what they discussed in your group time. Close this discussion in prayer.

Put on then, as God's chosen ones, holy and beloved, compassionate hearts, kindness, humility, meekness, and patience, bearing with one another and, if one has a complaint against another, forgiving each other; as the Lord has forgiven you, so you also must forgive. And above all these put on love, which binds everything together in perfect harmony. And let the peace of Christ rule in your hearts, to which indeed you were called in one body. And be thankful.

COLOSSIANS 3:12–15 ESV

PASSIONS :: 6

*God built us to love different things so
we could meet different needs.*

MAIN IDEA: God often leads us to passions through suffering experienced or perceived.

Here are some general goals and thoughts for your time together this week:

:: Passions are the needs you see around you or around the world that uniquely make your heart race or move you.

:: We are most fulfilled when we are meeting needs around us.

:: God prepared good works in advance for us to walk in. Dream about what those could be.

:: It is a privilege to participate in the work of God. What is holding you back?

:: There are two big passion killers: comparison and fear of man's approval. What does it look like to be free of those?

MAIN GOAL: To identify unique need that you are designed to meet and be moved by God to meet it.

HOMEWORK DISCUSSION

Here are some suggested places to focus as you go over the homework together. Ask the group:

:: What did you learn by studying Joseph's passions this week?

:: How did your view of the word *passion* change this week?

:: What passions arose in you as you worked through Project 1?

:: From Project 2, what does it look like to fight comparison and the fear of man?

:: What else did you learn as you studied and interacted with the lesson and Scripture this week?

VIDEO AND/OR TEACHING

Watch video session: *Passions*

ASK CONVERSATION CARDS

If you are in a large group, break into small groups of five for discussion time using the Ask conversation cards. Distribute this week's Ask cards and guide the women to ask and answer the questions on the cards. Remember to begin with the Scripture card and end by stressing the scriptural truth group members can apply to their lives as a result of what they discussed in your group time. Close this discussion in prayer.

For the joy set before him he endured the cross, scorning its shame, and sat down at the right hand of the throne of God. Consider him who endured such opposition from sinners, so that you will not grow weary and lose heart.

HEBREWS 12:2–3

MYSTERY :: 7

Nothing we have done matters without the Spirit of God.

MAIN IDEA: God's goal for our lives is that we would live in complete and utter surrender and dependence on him. He built us to need him. So our purposes are most likely fleshed out and revealed and lived moving closely with his Spirit.

Here are some general goals and thoughts for your time together this week:

- :: Lean into what you don't know as much as what you do know. God is in this with us. He doesn't reveal every detail of our lives, or we would not depend on him so desperately.

- :: He often moves through our weakness and fear more than our strength and confidence.

- :: The Spirit can move powerfully through the very most average of us.

- :: Life is best lived in relationship with Jesus: eyes fixed, heart simply in love with him and moved to obey him no matter the costs.

- :: None of our threads are all the same, which means we each must feel tremendous responsibility to steward our lives—and the threads God has given us—well.

MAIN GOAL: No matter what we know or don't know about our purposes, God is most after us in relationship with him.

HOMEWORK DISCUSSION

Here are some suggested places to focus as you go over the homework together. Ask the group:

:: As you studied the scriptures this week, what stood out to you?

:: As you look through the threads of your life, what stands out to you?

:: Break up into pairs and let your partner share what she sees as she studies the unique threads God has given her.

:: Share how your perspective has shifted since the first week.

VIDEO AND/OR TEACHING

Watch video session: *Mystery*

ASK CONVERSATION CARDS

If you are in a large group, break into small groups of five for discussion time using the Ask conversation cards. Distribute this week's Ask cards and guide the women to ask and answer the questions on the cards. Remember to begin with the Scripture card and end by stressing the scriptural truth group members can apply to their lives as a result of what they discussed in your group time. Close this discussion in prayer.

But the Advocate, the Holy Spirit, whom the Father will send in my name, will teach you all things and will remind you of everything I have said to you.

JOHN 14:26

HOW TO FIND GOD

I can't imagine a more restless feeling than being unsure about the meaning of life and the future of my soul. As long as we are on this earth, we will ache for something bigger, because we were designed for something bigger—something better. We are designed for an intimate relationship with God forever.

Saint Augustine said, "You have made us for yourself, and our hearts are restless until they find their rest in you."[1]

We had a perfect relationship with God until sin entered the world through Adam and Eve. And with sin came the promise of death and eternal separation from God. But from the moment of the first sin, God issued a promise that would bring us back to him.

The penalty had to be paid.

Our sin was to be placed on a perfect sacrifice. God would send his own blameless, perfect Son to bear our sin and suffer our fate—to get us back.

Jesus came fulfilling thousands of years of prophecy, lived a perfect life, and died a gruesome death, reconciling our payment for our sin. Then after three days, he defeated death and rose from the grave and now is seated with the Father, waiting for us.

---

1. Augustine of Hippo, *Saint Augustine's Confessions,* trans. Albert C. Outler (Mineola, N.Y.: Courier Dover Publications, 2002), 103.

Anyone who accepts the blood of Jesus for the forgiveness of their sin is adopted as a child of God, and issued God's very own Spirit to seal and empower us to live this life for him.

Our souls are restless until they rest in God. We were made for him, and he gave everything so that our souls could finally and forever rest in him.

If you have never trusted Christ for the forgiveness of your sins, you can do that this moment. Just tell him your need for him and tell him of your trust in him as your Lord and Savior.

ABOUT THE AUTHOR

JENNIE ALLEN is an award-winning and bestselling author of *Anything* and *Restless*, as well as the Bible studies *Stuck, Chase,* and *Restless.* The founder and visionary for the IF: Gathering, she is a passionate leader following God's call on her life to catalyze a generation of women to live what they believe. Jennie has a master's in biblical studies from Dallas Theological Seminary and lives in Austin, Texas, with her husband, Zac. Together they have been blessed with four children, the youngest of whom was adopted from Rwanda.

IF:GATHERING

GATHER
EQUIP
UNLEASH

IFGATHERING.COM

Also Available from
jennie allen

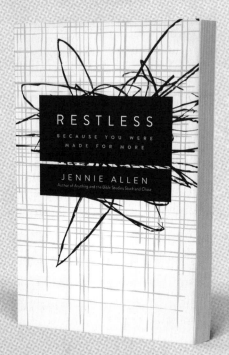

Identify the threads of your life

Using the story of Joseph, Jennie explains how his suffering, gifts, story, and relationships fit into the greater story of God—and how your story can do the same. She introduces Threads—a tool to help you see your own personal story and to uncover and understand the raw materials God has given you to use for his glory and purpose.

Visit **www.jennieallen.com** for info about *Restless.*

Available wherever books & Bibles are sold.

Also Available from
jennie allen

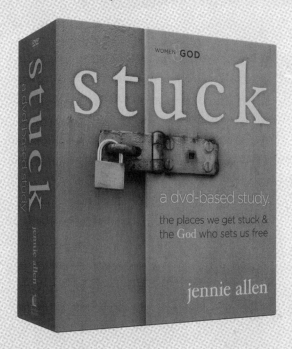

A New Bible Study Experience for Women

Women are hurting. A lot of us feel stuck. This is not a novel perception—this is human. We are stuck trying to be perfect. Stuck in sadness. Stuck feeling numb. Stuck pursuing more stuff to make us happy. Stuck in something we can't even name. *Stuck* is an eight-session Bible study experience leading women to the invisible struggles that we fight and to the God who has to set us free.

Visit **www.stuckdvdstudy.com** for learn more.

Available wherever books & Bibles are sold.

THOMAS NELSON
Since 1798

Also Available from
jennie allen

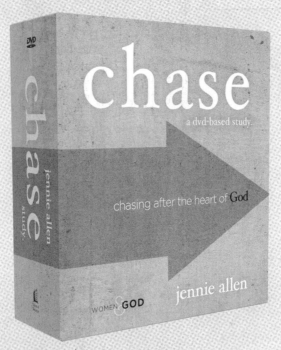

Chasing After the Heart of God

Chase is a Bible study experience to discover the heart of God and what it is exactly He wants from us. As we work through major events in the life of David, and the Psalms he wrote out of those experiences, you see a man who was reckless and imperfect but possessed the favor of God. Whether you are running from God or working your tail off to please Him, this man's journey will challenge your view of God.

Watch **www.jennieallen.com** for more info about *Chase*.

Available wherever books & Bibles are sold.